Around *My Mother's* Table

Around My Mother's Table

Stories and Recipes Celebrating Lives Lost to Breast Cancer

Compiled & Edited by
Lisa Burton

ISBN 1-58597-379-3

Library of Congress Control Number: 2006901293

A portion of the proceeds from sales of this book will be used to further breast cancer initiatives.

LEATHERS
PUBLISHING
4500 College Boulevard
Overland Park, Kansas 66211
1-888-888-7696
www.leatherspublishing.com

For my mother,
Carol Jean (McReynolds) Durbin,
1947  *2003,*
with enduring love.

Presented to:

_____

"A mother's love grows by giving."

 Nature often offers metaphors more elegant than any we can manufacture, and Muir Woods is no exception. Redwoods have evolved to turn disaster into opportunity. In these coastal forests, death produces life.

 This is what I mean: In the redwood ecosystem, buds for future trees are contained in pods called burls, tough brown knobs that cling to the bark of the mother tree. When the mother tree is logged, blown over or destroyed by fire – when, in other words, she dies – the trauma stimulates the burls' growth hormones. The seeds release, and trees sprout around her, creating the circle of daughters. The daughter trees grow by absorbing the sunlight their mother cedes to them when she dies. And they get the moisture and nutrients they need from their mother's root system, which remains intact underground even after her leaves die. Although the daughters exist independently of their mother above ground, they continue to draw sustenance from her underneath.

 I am fooling only myself when I say my mother exists now only in the photograph on my bulletin board or in the outline of my hand or in the armful of memories I still hold tight. She lives on beneath everything I do. Her presence influenced who I was, and her absence influences who I am. Our lives are shaped as much by those who leave us as they are by those who stay. Loss is our legacy. Insight is our gift. Memory is our guide.

– Excerpt from *Motherless Daughters* by Hope Edelman

Table of Contents

*M*y beautiful mom, Carol Durbin, died from complications caused by breast cancer on April 4, 2003. She was 54 and just starting to enjoy the "Grandma" phase of her life.

The experience of losing my mother had a profound effect on me, and I realized very early on that nothing in my life would ever be the same. As soon as the fog started to lift, I decided that I wanted to do something positive to help me get through the heartache I was feeling. I started a business called Pink Ribbon Connection, where I specialize in breast cancer awareness products, including jewelry, stained glass, hand-made cards and t-shirts. The appreciation that my customers express has been very rewarding – through them, I feel like I am making a difference in somebody's life, be it a cancer survivor, a daughter, a granddaughter, or a friend. I feel blessed that my work is helping to raise awareness of the enormous toll this disease has taken among the lives of the women we love.

You are holding the latest and, I feel, greatest Pink Ribbon Connection project – *Around My Mother's Table*, a collection of heirloom recipes, touching stories and family photos. This is a book intended to comfort. The recipes are from mothers who carried the instinctive need to bond with their children and families. The stories reflect the deep love a mother gives and receives by feeding her child's body and nourishing her child's soul. The photos reveal the beauty of our beloved mothers and our relationship with them.

As you read this book, I hope that you will find a recipe to share with your family, one that will nourish them and be cherished throughout the years. I hope your hearts are touched and you are inspired to pick up the phone to call your own mom. If that isn't possible, maybe you will pull out one of her "special" recipes and make it tonight as a celebration of her life!

This book would not have been possible without the wonderful, generous women and men who have shared a special part of their mothers with me. I extend a loving "thank you" to them and am forever grateful. This book has truly been a labor of love – I hope you treasure it!

– Lisa Burton

Velsa Agar

I lost my mother on March 24, 1982, 23 years ago. She was only 57. After her initial diagnosis of breast cancer in 1977, she showed us what a true Viking she really was. She had a radical mastectomy on December 19, 1977, and was determined to be home for Christmas Eve to cook her traditional Norwegian Christmas Dinner, and she did just that. She could not lift the pans in and out of the oven, but she was there directing me, then 26, to make the meal.

Every Christmas Eve, I still make her dinner and feel her spirit guiding my hand. Her Christmas tablecloth was given to me when I married in 1979, and this year it will adorn the table for the 53rd year. This tradition will pass on to my daughter, Alyssa, now 19. One of my strongest memories of Mama was her sense of humor; she never lost it.

After her surgery she used to say that there was no use crying over spilled milk. Or, why couldn't the doctors have removed both breasts, that way you could pick your size according to the occasion–for hot weather, a small cup size, for a formal affair, a large size or VAVOOM!! It still makes me laugh so many years later.

– From loving daughter,
Kristin Agar

Norwegian Christmas Dinner

Roast Loin of Pork   (prepared to your liking)
Pork Ribs   (prepared to your liking)
Roasted Potatoes   (prepared to your liking)
Surkahl   (Norwegian sauerkraut)
Fromage   (whipped cream dessert)

Surkahl

1 medium green cabbage
3 T. butter
3-4 T. caraway seeds
Water
1 C. white vinegar, or to taste
3 T. sugar, or to taste

- Cut the cabbage into quarters. Remove core and cut into thin strips.
- Melt butter in large pot. Brown cabbage in melted butter.
- As cabbage browns, add caraway seeds.
- When cabbage is partly browned, cover with water and bring to a boil. Turn heat down and simmer about 1 hour.
- Turn heat back up to low and add vinegar and sugar. If still too tart, add a bit more sugar.

When serving, spoon into a serving dish with a slotted spoon so as not to serve all of the liquid. Will taste even better the second day when reheated.

(Continued...)

Fromage

2 C. whipping cream
1 T. sugar
Fresh fruit (your choice, don't use kiwi or
pineapple – gelatin won't set properly)
2 envelopes Knox gelatin

- Whip the cream with the sugar.
- Add fruit to whipped cream.
- Dissolve gelatin as directed.
- Fold into whipped cream/fruit mixture.
- Put in refrigerator to set overnight.

This is a VERY rich dessert. Thanks for letting me share part of
my mother with you!

– Recipes from the Kitchen of Velsa Agar

Anna Jean
Armato

All of my mother's cooking was incredible due to the one special ingredient she consistently used – sprinkles of love. Whether she was cooking for my teammates on the football team or our intimate holiday get-togethers, Mom would get up early to start the preparation. My Nana and Papa from the old neighborhood would come over, along with Mom's twin brother and sister, Carl and Patty, who would fly in from out of town. Other local extended family would usually total around 20, and would be welcomed by Mom's special embrace and the words she lived by, "The more the merrier!" Mom, being the family glue and the reason why holidays even happened, was a shining example of being attentive to detail and of impeccable planning.

It's so difficult to pinpoint just one of Mom's recipes to share, as her extensive menus almost merit their own publication. The thing with Mom was that she would not just give you her recipe – she would invite you over to teach you in person how to prepare the dish. Then she would sit down and enjoy it with you.

Though I was the only child, my house, especially the kitchen, was always filled with my friends who adored Mom. Her welcoming smile and hugs were the best things in her kitchen. Mom and I would always enjoy a cup of coffee while visiting in the kitchen as she cooked. She would stop here and there to make eye contact as she shared her motherly advice for her son's woes of life as a young man. We cherished our time together and those memories are something I will pass along to my daughters, Anna and Ava, about their Nana Anna (on right in photo, with my Nana) and how she used to live life with that one special ingredient – love – in all that she did.

– From loving son,
Frank Armato

Anna's Italian Chicken Spedini

5 lbs. boneless, skinless chicken strips
6 eggs, well beaten
7 C. Italian breadcrumbs
Mogu Sauce (recipe follows)

- Dip each chicken strip into the beaten eggs and then into the breadcrumbs, coating well.
- Roll each breaded strip up tightly and place a long metal skewer through it; 5 to 7 strips should fit on each skewer.
- Baste the chicken with the sauce, saving extra sauce to serve at the table.
- Cook on a hot grill, turning the skewers frequently until the chicken strips are golden brown. Serve immediately.

Mogu Sauce

4 C. olive oil
½ C. lemon juice
1½ C. water
3 cloves garlic, crushed
1 C. grated Romano cheese

– Recipe from the Kitchen of Anna Jean Armato

"All that I am or hope to be I owe to my mother."

– Abraham Lincoln

Betty Brawner

What can I say about my mother, Betty? She was a little four-foot ball of fire with personality plus. She had her own business, Betty Brawner Associates Interior Design, and it felt like she knew everybody in Kansas City. I couldn't go anywhere that someone who knew Mom didn't recognize me. So I didn't get away with much! Business-wise, she was a real go-getter and occasionally even had to turn business away. She wasn't home very much when I was in middle school. During the day, she was at her store and during the evenings, she was at clients' homes and wouldn't get home until about 11:00 p.m. when I was already out like a light. I did see her in the mornings before school. Dad would have breakfast ready for us girls, take coffee and the paper up to Mom in bed, and then he'd leave for work. After we ate, we would jump into bed with Mom for a bit before we had to get ready for school. That was our favorite time.

Mom was a very hard-working woman and is missed by all. My oldest child, Nathan, can remember her and my middle child, Rachel, has a few memories, but my youngest, Brandon, doesn't remember her at all. I wish my children had been able to spend more time with her because we all know how special grandmothers are to kids. I know my grandmother was my favorite person in the world.

Mom's meatloaf was our favorite dish. I have given this recipe out hundreds of times and I make it for my family at least once a month. My husband says some of the restaurants around town need to get Mom's recipe. The sauce really adds to the meatloaf, and we all love cold meatloaf sandwiches with extra sauce added the next day!

– From loving daughter,
Beve Freeman

Meatloaf

⅔ C. dry bread crumbs
2 C. milk
2 eggs, beaten
¼ C. chopped onion
1 t. salt
⅛ t. ground sage
1½ lb. ground beef
Sauce (recipe follows)

- Preheat oven to 350°.
- Soak bread crumbs in the milk. Add the eggs, onion, salt and sage and mix well.
- Add the ground beef to the bread crumb mixture and blend thoroughly with hands. Place meat in a loaf pan and bake for 1 hour.
- Combine sauce ingredients and refrigerate until ready to use.
- When meatloaf is cooked through, drain liquid off and spoon sauce on top.
- Bake another 10 minutes.
- Serve with extra sauce.

Sauce

¼ t. nutmeg
1 t. dry mustard
¼ C. ketchup
3 T. brown sugar

– Recipe from the Kitchen of Betty Brawner

Florine Ball
Callaway

I lost my mother, Florine Ball Callaway, to breast cancer in 1974. I very much cherish all the lessons of life she passed on to me. I have always enjoyed cooking, which was one of the things she taught me to do. I was also diagnosed with breast cancer in 1979 and again in 1997. Today I am a survivor and doing well. The important things to remember are to always think positively, cook well and enjoy every day of life!

– From loving daughter,
Dorothy Callaway Isdell

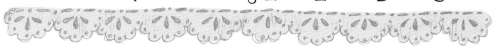

Ham Loaf

2 lbs. ground cured ham
2 lbs. ground fresh pork
4 eggs, slightly beaten
1½ C. whole sweet milk
2½ C. crushed graham crackers
Ham Loaf Sauce (recipe follows)

- Preheat oven to 300°.
- Mix together the ham loaf ingredients and place in a 9" x 13" greased loaf pan.
- Mix together the sauce ingredients and spread over the ham loaf.
- Bake for 2 hours or until done.

Ham Loaf Sauce

1 can tomato soup
1 C. brown sugar
1 t. prepared mustard
½ C. water
½ C. vinegar

– Recipe from the Kitchen of Florine Ball Callaway

"A mother is she who can take the place of all others, but whose place no one else can take."

– Cardinal Mermillod

Virginia Calvin

My parents, Lloyd and Virginia Calvin, moved from Kansas City, Missouri, to Atlanta, Georgia, with their two young children (Becky, 5 [me] and Michael, 2) in 1946, just a few months prior to the birth of their third child, Jimmy. They very quickly became enamored with the Southern lifestyle, including Southern cooking, and would soon forsake their Midwestern culinary background for – to them – the more exotic dishes of the South. So we kids were raised on the delicious recipes my mother received from our many friends and neighbors in Atlanta.

I so often remember coming home from school and walking through our front door to be greeted with the most marvelous aromas coming from the kitchen. Mother loved cooking and, whether she was baking cakes or dinner for company or just for our family, she always did it with panache. I adored being in the kitchen with her and she, I think, loved having me there. She made fabulous fried chicken and when Daddy would come into the kitchen and ask, "What's cookin', good lookin'?", she would always answer with a twinkle in her eye, "Chicken, wanna neck?", and we would all just laugh.

Like all families, when a loved one is diagnosed with a terrible disease, we were devastated to hear of her breast cancer. She fought bravely, never complaining, and for a while we thought she might have beaten this monster. But she was not one of the lucky ones; nor were we.

There are so many things I miss about my mother, but I especially wish I had asked more questions regarding her culinary specialties. Like many good cooks, she often created dishes by memory or intuition rather than from recipes. I have a few of her favorites, written in her hand, but not nearly enough. The recipe I'm sharing here, a family favorite, is a chicken dish called "Country Captain." Mother cooked this dish for special occasions and would serve it with great style and lots of love.

– From loving daughter,
Becky Calvin Robinson

Country Captain

½ C. flour
¼ t. salt
⅛ t. ground black pepper
4½ - 5 lbs. chicken breast halves
  (bone in, skin removed)
3 T. vegetable shortening (plus more if needed)
2 medium onions, diced
2 medium green bell peppers, diced
2 cloves garlic, minced
4 C. coarsely chopped tomatoes (fresh or canned)
⅛ C. finely chopped parsley (plus more for garnish)
1 t. dried thyme
2 t. Worcestershire sauce
1 T. hot curry powder
Salt and freshly ground black pepper, to taste
½ C. currants
Slivered almonds, toasted (for garnish)

(Continued...)

- Mix together the flour, salt and pepper in a large shallow bowl.
- Dredge the chicken breasts in the seasoned flour and shake off excess.
- In a large frying pan, over medium heat, melt the shortening and brown the chicken until tender and just golden, turning frequently. (This can be done in two batches.) Remove chicken from the pan and set aside.
- In same pan, with heat turned down a bit, sauté the onions, bell peppers and garlic until softened. Add the tomatoes, parsley, thyme, Worcestershire sauce, curry powder and salt and pepper to taste. Simmer at least 30 minutes on medium-low heat.
- While sauce is cooking, preheat oven to 325°.
- Place chicken pieces in a large, shallow baking dish and spread with the tomato sauce. Cover the baking dish and cook for 30 minutes; uncover the chicken and bake another 15 minutes, or until chicken is cooked through. Remove from oven.
- Stir in the currants and sprinkle with extra parsley and the almonds. Serve immediately and enjoy!

– Recipe from the Kitchen of Virginia Calvin

My mother was the making of me. She was so true and so sure of me. I felt that I had someone to live for — someone I must not disappoint. The memory of my mother will always be a blessing to me!

– Thomas Edison

Arline Downes

Mom was in relatively good health before the discovery of her cancer, so I feel that with earlier detection she might still be alive today. Her breast cancer was discovered in 1986. A mastectomy was done and the nodes were checked; no cancer appeared to be left. At that time, the process did not call for any further treatment other than yearly checks. Five years later, Mom's cancer returned with a vengeance, and by then it had attacked her bones. She subsequently endured many chemo and radiation treatments, giving her a few good years with us. And even though she was otherwise an extremely strong lady, the cancer eventually won out.

For the past 20 years I have lived in Florida, and during the time my mom was alive, she spent every winter with me. Her doctors would arrange it so that she could take treatments while visiting me. Her chemo was always scheduled on Monday mornings. It was not until Tuesday evenings that she would become ill, so after her treatments I would put her in a wheelchair and off to the mall we would go. Lunch was always first on our list, and then we would browse the stores. I am so thankful God gave me this time with my mom, as it was then I discovered how much alike we were.

This is not a fancy recipe, but it is what I call "comfort food." When I feel sad or blue, it makes me think of my mom. The last time I made this recipe, I actually broke my wooden spoon while stirring the batter. I laughed until tears rolled down my cheeks because I knew Mom was with me, somewhere laughing just as hard as I was.

A few days before my mother died, she asked my cousin, "What will poor Mary do without me?" My cousin assured her that I was also a strong lady; but like her cookies, I will never be quite as strong!

– From loving daughter,
Mary Chamberlain

Soft Molasses Cookies

1 C. sugar
2 t. baking soda
1 t. salt
1½ t. ground ginger
½ t. ground cloves
1 C. shortening
1 C. molasses
1 egg
1 C. hot coffee
Flour sufficient to work with

- Preheat oven to 375°.
- In a large bowl, blend together the sugar, baking soda, salt, ginger and cloves.
- In a medium bowl, cream together the shortening, molasses, egg and coffee.
- Stir the wet ingredients into the dry ingredients and blend well.
- Then, add the flour. The flour is the secret to these cookies! My mom always added flour by the cup until she could not stir the batter with a wooden spoon anymore. Her arms were definitely much stronger than mine! I push myself to add the flour until the batter is very stiff (trying not to break any more wooden spoons in the process!).
- Drop by tablespoon onto a lightly greased cookie sheet and bake for 10 minutes. Cool on rack and enjoy!

(Special hint – Mom would sometimes add raisins to these cookies and call them "Hermits"!)

– Recipe from the Kitchen of Arline Downes

Carol Durbin

My mom, Carol Durbin, was no Betty Crocker. Cooking was not one of her favorite pastimes, but when she did cook, it was always good. She loved going out to eat, so if she had her way she would have had every dinner at a nice restaurant. I do have fond memories of Mom cooking some things such as goulash, hamburger soup and chocolate sheet cake. It was always a treat when she did decide to cook. Unfortunately, I inherited my mom's non-cooking genes!

The recipe I chose to submit is not a family "heirloom" recipe, but it is the last thing that I ever cooked with my mom. It was Christmas morning of 2002. I was well aware that Mom was sick, but I never imagined that it would be her last Christmas. I was assigned breakfast duty and decided to make Bacon and Cheese Quiche.

After opening our gifts, Mom and I headed to the kitchen to cook. I was 29 years old and had never prepared a quiche before, so Mom walked me through it step-by-step. We stood in the kitchen in our jammies, beating eggs, chopping veggies, frying bacon and filling pie shells. I anticipated the look on everyone's faces when they took their first bite of my yummy Bacon and Cheese Quiche. No one could believe that I had made it and, as my mother often did, she  gave me full credit. I will always cherish the memory of my wonderful mom and that last Christmas morning that we spent together in the kitchen. I love you and miss you, Mom!

– From loving daughter,
Michelle Campbell

Bacon & Cheese Quiche

½ lb. bacon
1 large onion, chopped
2 eggs, beaten
1 T. all-purpose flour
½ t. salt
Pepper to taste
1 C. milk
2 C. shredded cheddar cheese
Sliced mushrooms
1 9-inch pie shell

- Preheat oven to 450°.
- Fry the bacon until crisp. Remove from skillet, drain and crumble. Discard all but 1 T. of the grease.
- Reheat the skillet with remaing 1 T. of grease over medium heat. Add the onion and sauté for about 5 minutes; do not brown.
- Place the beaten eggs in a medium bowl and add the flour, salt and pepper. Add the milk and beat until well blended. Add the cheese, mushrooms, bacon and onion and stir.
- Pour quiche mixture into the pie shell. Bake for 10 minutes, then reduce the oven temperature to 350° and continue baking for about 20 minutes, until a knife blade inserted in the center comes out clean.
- Remove from oven and let stand for 10 minutes. Cut into wedges and serve warm.

– Recipe from the Kitchen of Carol Durbin

(Continued...)

Homemade pizza, big stuffed burritos, Hamburger Helper and breakfast for dinner are a few of the dishes that I recall when I think about my mom, Carol Durbin, in the kitchen. My mom never really developed a flair for gourmet cooking or baking. She was about simple fare and spending time with her family around the dinner table at the end of the day. The one thing about cooking that my mom did love was collecting cookbooks. I can still picture her sitting at the kitchen table with her reading glasses resting low on her nose, thumbing through her newest cookbook. I have inherited a small collection of her cookbooks, and the rest of them are still sitting in the kitchen cabinet right where she left them. Most of them are unused but all well loved.

The recipe I have chosen is one that I didn't begin to love until after I was married. My parents frequently had my husband and I over for dinner in the early years of our marriage. One night my mom served "Hamburger Soup" with bread and butter, and my husband was hooked! I know my mom was pleased by the fact that she "had a dish" that we all had such an appetite for. Now, each time I make "Hamburger Soup" for my family, I take my time and make it with love just as she did.

But to no avail, because after the first bite the response is always the same ... my husband very tenderly says, "It's good honey, but it's not your mom's." That's okay with me!

– From loving daughter,
Lisa Burton

30

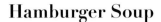

Hamburger Soup

1½ lb. ground beef
½ C. chopped onion
1 C. cubed potatoes
1 16-oz. pkg. frozen peas and carrots
1 C. shredded cabbage
1 28-oz. can diced tomatoes, undrained
1 small bay leaf
Salt to taste
⅛ t. black pepper
2 C. water
2 14½-oz. cans beef broth
1 t. kitchen bouquet

- In soup pot, cook ground beef and onion over medium-high heat until beef is brown and onion is tender, stirring occasionally; drain.
- Add all other ingredients. Cover and simmer for one hour. (Soup is ready to serve after 30 minutes, but flavor is enhanced after longer cooking.)

– Recipe from the Kitchen of Carol Durbin

"To have a loving mother is one of the best of God's good gifts."

– Anonymous

Joan Everson

I miss my mom a lot. She was not only my mom, but my best friend as well. She was one of the few people I could talk to about anything. We always enjoyed spending quality time together, whether it was cooking, shopping or any of the many other things we enjoyed. My mom was a very caring and loving person, especially when it came to my dad, my three older brothers and myself.

I am truly thankful that God has left us with a spiritual connection with each other. There are times when I really need her and I know she is with me in spirit. Though some people may not believe it, because of the strong spiritual connection we have, my mom has helped me deal with her death and get on with my life. I know that now she is in a better place and is no longer suffering.

I can't believe she has been gone for 10 years. Christmas is one of the hardest times of the year for me because she used to buy me something really special as one of my presents. My mom was only 56 when she passed away and she fought the cancer for eight years. I don't know how she did it for so long. She was such a strong person, stronger than I would have been. I think what kept Mom going was my dad, brothers, her grandchildren, and me. With everything she went through, she still put all of us first all the way to the end, no matter how much pain she was going through.

On Mom's last night on earth, she was worried that she was a burden on us. I remember my dad telling her that it was our turn to take care of her. There is nothing in the world that I would not have done for her or do for my dad, brothers, nieces and nephews. I feel that if you don't have family, you have nothing.

– From loving daughter,
Monica Stansberry

This recipe is a family tradition for holiday dinners. My mom always made it for Thanksgiving and Christmas. I think of her whenever I make it.

Slush Punch

3 C. boiling water
1 C. sugar
3 oz. package of Jell-O
  (recommended flavors: cherry, lemon, or pineapple)
1 46-48 oz. can Dole pineapple juice
2-liter bottle of soda pop
  (recommended flavors: Sprite, Mountain Dew,
  or orange)

- Mix together the water, sugar, Jell-O, and pineapple juice and freeze for two days.
- Before serving, allow mixture to thaw slightly in refrigerator for 3-4 hours.
- Crush or break up the semi-frozen mixture into a large punch bowl and add a 2-liter bottle of soda pop. (I recommend either Sprite with cherry Jell-O, Mountain Dew with lemon Jell-O, or orange with pineapple Jell-O.)

(Continued...)

Butterscotch Pudding

¾ C. brown sugar
3 T. cornstarch
½ t. salt
¾ C. water
1¼ C. milk
¼ C. butter
2 eggs
1 t. vanilla
Graham cracker pie crust (optional)

- Mix together the brown sugar, cornstarch, salt, water, milk and butter, and cook in a saucepan over medium heat, stirring constantly, until mixture thickens and boils for 1 minute. Remove from heat.
- In a separate bowl, slightly beat the eggs and add ½ of the hot mixture, stirring well.
- Blend the egg mixture with the remaining hot mixture in the saucepan. Boil 1 minute longer, stirring constantly.
- Remove from heat and stir in the vanilla. Blend well.
- Pour the pudding into a graham cracker pie crust or into serving cups and refrigerate until set and chilled.

– Recipes from the Kitchen of Joan Everson

Jane Graham

This recipe was and still is one of our family's favorites! My mom would make this casserole at Thanksgiving and Christmas. She was a wonderful cook and baker, always making everything from scratch. She baked bread once a week and with that came fresh cinnamon rolls, fry bread and pizza dough to make homemade pizzas. She made apple, pumpkin, pecan and strawberry pies, much to my dad's delight. My brother and I had favorite cookies and bars that she would make for us after school. She loved to be in the kitchen and taught me at a young age how to bake and cook. I learned a great deal from her and have her recipe box to refer to whenever I need it.

– From loving daughter,
Sally Reuer

Green Bean Casserole

6 T. margarine
1 small green pepper, diced
1 small jar pimentos, chopped
1 can cream of mushroom soup
1 can evaporated milk
1 jar Old English cheese
3 cans French-style green beans, drained
1 sleeve of Ritz crackers, crumbled

- Preheat oven to 350°.
- Melt margarine in a skillet. Add green pepper and pimentos. Cook until tender.
- Meanwhile, heat cream of mushroom soup, milk and Old English cheese in a saucepan.
- Add soup mixture to green pepper mixture; blend well and then mix in the green beans. Heat until warm.
- Place mixture in a casserole dish and sprinkle Ritz crackers over the top.
- Bake for 30 minutes or until casserole is bubbling. (This dish can be made ahead of time, refrigerated and cooked later.)

– Recipe from the Kitchen of Jane Graham

"The mother's heart is the child's schoolroom."

– Henry Ward Beecher

Betty Lou
Holloway

My mom loved to cook! She would make pies from scratch, using fruit from the trees and bushes in our yard. She would bake up tons of oatmeal cookies and fried chicken and send them to our uncle in Texas. My grandfather owned a quail and pheasant farm and Mom created a special cookbook for his farm. This recipe is from that booklet.

When my parents were first married, Mom didn't know anything about cooking (not even how to boil water, according to Dad!). They loved to eat fine food, but had little money on a teacher's salary. So Mom taught herself to cook and eventually even had a small cable cooking show.

Mom taught me confidence through cooking. She had me cook lobster tails when I was only twelve. I was so scared because they were such a special treat, but Mom trusted me. She showed me everything to do and didn't ever get stressed or yell. I was so proud of that dinner! Mom also decided we should try to make Beef Wellington together. It took us two days to cook it from scratch. She took me to a chefs' association meeting and I was in line behind two chefs who were talking about always wanting to make Beef Wellington but being too nervous to try it. Knowing that Mom and I had made it when I was only fourteen gave me such confidence.

I was thirteen when Mom first got breast cancer. And she survived – even thrived – for nine years before it struck again. I lost Mom when I was 23, but the courage and confidence she taught me through cooking will stay with me forever. Someday I will hopefully pass it on to the granddaughters she never got to meet.

– From loving daughter,
Mary Putnam

Roast Pheasant with Wild Rice Stuffing

2 lb. pheasant
1 stick butter
½ C. chopped onion
½ C. chopped celery
2 T. chopped parsley
2 t. salt
¼ t. freshly ground pepper
¼ t. ground thyme
1½ t. dried sage
2½ C. wild rice
½ C. chicken stock (or more as needed)

- Preheat oven to 350°.
- Thoroughly salt and pepper the pheasant inside and out, then set aside and prepare the stuffing.
- Melt the butter in a skillet. Add the onions and celery and lightly sauté. Add the parsley, salt, pepper, thyme and sage and mix well.
- Wash and drain the wild rice, cover generously with the chicken stock in a medium saucepan and simmer 20 minutes.
- Add the onion mixture in with the rice and continue to simmer until most of the liquid has been absorbed and rice is firm, about 10 minutes more.
- Pack the bird's cavity with the wild rice stuffing. Place in roasting pan and cook for approximately 90 minutes, or until bird is golden. (If you choose to serve an unstuffed pheasant, roast for about 60 minutes and serve stuffing on the side.)

– *Recipe from the Kitchen of Betty Lou Holloway*

YOUR MOTHER IS ALWAYS WITH YOU

Your mother is always with you...
She's the whisper of the leaves
As you walk down the street.
She's the smell of bleach
in your freshly laundered socks.
She's the cool hand on your brow
When you're not well.
Your mother lives inside your laughter.
She's crystallized in every tear drop.
She's the place you came from,
Your first home...
She's the map you follow
With every step that you take.
She's your first love
And your first heart break...
And nothing on earth can separate you...
Not time, not space
Not even death
Will ever separate you from your mother...
You carry her inside of you.

— Author Unknown

Ellen Edmondson House

Ellen Edmondson House was the mother of three girls: Georgia, Charlotte and Margaret. She is remembered by all who knew her as compassionate, fun-loving and thoughtful.

Her rolls were the talk of the town come Christmas time! She would spend days in the kitchen preparing the homemade gifts for friends, neighbors, dentists, doctors, teachers…anyone who touched our lives. I even remember climbing onto the school bus with a pan of rolls and a card for my bus driver. To this day, we still have people tell us that rolls have never melted in their mouths the way Ellen's did.

Our mom had a real spirited side to her as well. If her girls were involved with an activity, a group of friends or even just an afternoon play date, Mrs. House was there! It's amazing to think about how she was able to juggle her volunteer work, her home and her disease while always making each one of us believe we were the center of her world. Perhaps her "Hunter's Stew" recipe was one of her secrets in playing Super Mom. A quick and simple recipe provided all of us with a healthy meal and full tummies. Afterward, she would take us out to enjoy ice cream, visit our beloved grandmother or even to play a harmless prank on a friend. She definitely had a spirited side!

Mama kept the holidays steeped in tradition. Her birthday was at the same time of the year as Thanksgiving, so we celebrated both occasions together. We submit these recipes in loving memory of our mother, who taught us – by her own example – strength of character, love for others and courage in the face of the most trying times. We love her and miss her!

– From loving daughters,
Georgia House Collier, Charlotte House and Margaret House

Ellen's Rolls

½ C. boiling water
½ C. shortening
¼ C. sugar
¾ t. salt
1 egg
1 yeast cake
½ C. cold water
3 C. unsifted all-purpose flour

- In a large mixing bowl, pour the boiling water over the shortening, sugar and salt. Blend and cool.
- Add the egg and stir to mix together.
- In a small bowl, let yeast stand in the cold water for 5 minutes, then stir and add to the egg mixture.

(Continued...)

- Add the flour in small amounts. Blend well, cover and place in refrigerator for at least 4 hours. (Dough must be in a mixing bowl large enough to allow it to double in size when rising later. It will keep in the refrigerator a week to 10 days.)
- About 3 hours before baking, roll the dough into desired shapes, using enough flour to handle easily. Place on a buttered pan and allow to double in size at room temperature.
- Bake in hot 425° oven for 12 to 15 minutes.

Hunter's Stew

2 T. bacon grease
2 medium onions, chopped
1 lb. ground beef
2 cans vegetable soup
4 slices American cheese, shredded

- Cook the onions in hot bacon grease in a large saucepan.
- Add the ground beef and brown thoroughly.
- Add the vegetable soup and stir well.
- Sprinkle with the American cheese.
- Simmer for 30 to 40 minutes.

Lemon Bisque

1 C. boiling water
1 package lemon Jell-O
¾ C. sugar
Juice from 3 lemons
Zest from 2 lemons
1 large can evaporated milk (chilled thoroughly)
Prepared pie shell
Whipped cream and canned cherries (optional)

- In a medium glass mixing bowl, pour the boiling water over the Jell-O, sugar, lemon juice and lemon zest. Stir until dissolved. Let sit until mixture begins to jell.
- In another glass mixing bowl, whip the evaporated milk until stiff peaks form.
- Fold the lemon mixture into the whipped milk and stir to blend.
- Pour mixture into the pie shell and refrigerate to set. (Can be served with a topping of whipped cream and cherries if desired.)

– Recipes from the Kitchen of Ellen Edmondson House

My mom's sugar cookie recipe holds such wonderful memories for me. She and I would make these delicious cookies together every year at Christmas time. We had so much fun rolling them out, cutting them into shapes and decorating them. We would then deliver them to family, friends and neighbors. We loved making these cookies just as much as everyone loved eating them!

Even though my mother has been gone for almost thirteen years, I still make her sugar cookies every Christmas. I use her handwritten recipe, her stainless steel mixing bowl and her cutout molds.

Now I have three little helpers of my own – Jacob (6), Joshua (4), and Emma (2) – who love to make Grandma Mary's sugar cookies as much as I do. When we make them together, I know I am creating a special memory with my children – it is a little piece of my mom that I can share with them. They all agree that Grandma Mary's cookies really are "The Best Sugar Cookies Ever!"

– From loving daughter,
Brandy Scrogham

The Best Sugar Cookies Ever

1 C. butter, softened
2 C. sugar
4 eggs
2 t. vanilla
4½ C. flour
1 t. baking powder
1 t. baking soda
1 t. salt

- Preheat oven to 350°.
- In a large mixing bowl, cream together the butter and sugar until smooth.
- Add the eggs and vanilla and beat mixture until light and fluffy.
- In a medium mixing bowl, stir together the flour, baking powder, baking soda and salt.
- Gradually add the flour mixture into the butter mixture, stirring well to combine.
- On a floured board, thickly roll out the cookie dough and cut into shapes using your favorite cutout molds or cookie cutters.
- Place on cookie sheets and bake in hot oven for 8 minutes.
- Remove immediately from cookie sheets and let cool on wire racks. (If desired, you may sprinkle with decorative toppings or frost with your favorite icing before serving.)

– Recipe from the Kitchen of Mary Jacobs

Sylvia Poad
Kamphaus

My mother-in-law, Sylvia Poad Kamphaus, was an excellent cook. She had many cookbooks and loved trying new things. Happily, I inherited them and love to read the handwritten notes in the margins. She made "Pizza by the Mile" for my husband and me in our early married life, and it has always been a family favorite. Two of my children have flown the nest and both have ended up calling to ask, "What is the recipe for 'Pizza by the Mile'?" Well, here it is!

– From loving daughter-in-law,
Candyce Kamphaus

Pizza by the Mile

1 long loaf of French bread, cut in half, then each
section sliced in half (to make four sections)
1 lb. lean ground beef
1 12-oz. can tomato paste
1 t. Italian seasoning
Sliced fresh tomatoes
American cheese, sliced diagonally

- Preheat oven to 375°.
- Brown the beef in a skillet over medium-high heat and drain off fat.
- Mix in the tomato paste and Italian seasoning, stirring to blend.
- Spread the meat mixture over the French bread slices, covering the entire surface of each.
- Add the tomato slices, alternating with a diagonal slice of cheese. (You will probably use 4 of each on each slice of French bread.)
- Bake until cheese is melted. It is YUMMY!

– Recipe from the Kitchen of Sylvia Poad Kamphaus

"Chance made you my mother-in-law;
Love made you my friend."

– Anonymous

LaVerne Kimber

My mother, LaVerne Kimber, was a shining example of all that a mother should be. She was such an influence for good in the lives of her eight children, 32 grandchildren and a growing number of great-grandchildren. Mom loved to sew and quilt. For many years, each grandchild would receive a handmade pair of pajamas for Christmas, and the adults in the family would receive hand-sewn items or even quilts. Grandma Kimber's presents were the only ones that could be opened on Christmas Eve. Birthdays and weddings were also made special by Mom's treasured gifts.

Mom was a wonderful cook. The family loved to gather for the delicious meals she prepared and these rolls were always a special treat. I remember them most at Thanksgiving time, when she would make dozens of them. I have made this recipe many times for my own family and always think of Mom when I do.

Whether it was cooking, sewing, gardening, listening, counseling or teaching, Mom added love to whatever she did, and that made all the difference.

– From loving daughter,
Diane Critchlow

Do-Ahead Dinner Rolls

1 C. milk
¼ C. margarine
1 package yeast
1 T. sugar
¼ C. lukewarm water
3 eggs
¼ C. sugar
2 t. salt
4 C. flour
Cooking oil
Melted margarine

- In a small saucepan, scald the milk over high heat. Add the margarine, stir to dissolve, and let the mixture cool.
- In a small bowl, combine the yeast and sugar in the lukewarm water.
- In a large mixing bowl, beat the eggs until light and fluffy. Add the sugar and salt, and blend well.
- Stir in the milk and yeast mixtures. Gradually add in the flour and mix well.
- Place in a warm spot and let rise until doubled in size. Punch dough down and grease the top with a little cooking oil. Cover and place dough in refrigerator overnight.
- On a floured board, roll dough out to about ⅜" thickness. Cut out rolls with a 2" round biscuit cutter. Stretch the cut-out dough and dip in melted margarine, then fold over to form a roll and place on a greased baking sheet to rise for 2-3 hours.
- Bake at 375° for 10-15 minutes, or until golden brown.

– Recipe from the Kitchen of LaVerne Kimber

Gloria Lloyd

Picnic meals are what I remember most about my mother, who died when I was five years old. We lived in Southern California, where the climate is nearly ideal for outdoor daily activity, so my mother served most of our meals picnic-style: breakfast, lunch and dinner. Whether it was in our backyard or at the local park, beach or nearby playground, all were frequent backdrops for family meals. Deviled eggs, or variations of this recipe, were part of the regular bill of fare, and also part of the food styling she created with each meal. The eggs might be circling around the ham on a big platter, or presented in their own design such as the shape of a bunny for Easter or a big smiling face amidst other condiments. Sometimes she would add food coloring to the yolks to match table décor and paper goods.

My mother made every meal a special event with an added touch to brighten the table or serve as a conversation piece. One time she served salads in large abalone shells rather than bowls, and another time she made green mashed potatoes for St. Patrick's Day. But it really didn't matter if there was a holiday to celebrate – she treated every meal as if it was a significant event.

Sure, deviled eggs make me think of my mother, but more than anything the food for thought is how she made the simplest of things special. It is as if she truly lived in the "now" and made the best of every day, regardless of the holiday or season. Just

remembering this has helped me celebrate life daily.

I don't wait for her birthday, Mother's Day or her death anniversary to honor my mother. Through my practice of honoring each day as special, I am also honoring her.

– From loving daughter,
Jill Lloyd

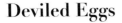

Deviled Eggs

6 hard-cooked eggs
¼ t. salt
2 T. sour cream
1 T. mayonnaise
1 t. prepared mustard
Dash of black pepper
Paprika

- Remove eggshells, and cut the cooked eggs in half lengthwise with a wet knife.
- Remove the yolks, being careful to keep whites intact.
- Place the yolks in a small bowl and thoroughly mash with a fork.
- Add the salt, sour cream, mayonnaise, mustard and pepper, and beat until fluffy.
- Refill the egg whites with the yolk mixture. Sprinkle with paprika and chill until ready to serve.

(Continued...)

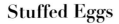

Stuffed Eggs

1 dozen hard-cooked eggs
1 C. flaked, cooked crab meat
1 C. finely chopped celery
2 T. chopped green pepper
1 T. French salad dressing mix
¼ C. mayonnaise or ⅓ C. sour cream

- Remove the eggshells and with a wet knife, slice the eggs in half lengthwise. Remove the yolks and finely mash them.
- Mix the mashed yolks with the crabmeat, celery and green pepper.
- Combine the salad dressing mix with mayonnaise and add to egg yolks; mix well.
- Pile mixture into the egg white halves and chill before serving.

– Recipes from the Kitchen of Gloria Lloyd

God made a wonderful mother,
A mother who never grows old.
He made her smile of the sunshine,
And he molded her heart of pure gold.
In her eyes He placed bright shining stars,
In her cheeks fair roses you see.
God made a wonderful mother,
And He gave that dear mother to me.

– Pat O'Reilly

Marie Mazurek

My dear mother, Marie Mazurek, was a good Christian woman who raised three daughters. She lost her battle with breast cancer twelve years ago.

She was one of those stay-at-home moms who had only her husband's income with which to work but who really enjoyed cooking, even though she had a tight budget.

She was always willing to share her tasty recipes with anyone who asked. I especially enjoy this "Chicken Gourmet" recipe and each time I cook it, I recall fond memories of my mother in the kitchen.

– From loving daughter,
Verna Neitz

Chicken Gourmet

1 fryer chicken, cut up
Salt, pepper and paprika to taste
6 T. shortening
¼ lb. fresh mushrooms, sliced
1 can artichoke hearts, drained
2 T. flour
3 T. sherry
¼ t. dried rosemary
⅔ C. chicken broth
Cooked rice

- Sprinkle chicken pieces with salt, pepper and paprika.
- Brown in 4 T. shortening and remove to casserole dish.
- Add remaining 2 T. shortening to the drippings and sauté the mushrooms.
- Arrange artichoke hearts in between chicken pieces.
- Sprinkle flour over the mushrooms and stir in the sherry, rosemary and chicken broth. Simmer for 10 minutes, then pour over the chicken.
- Cover and bake at 375° for 40 minutes. Serve over rice.

– Recipe from the Kitchen of Marie Mazurek

Joan Ellen
Denton Meador

Sometimes we are fortunate enough to have people in our lives who leave a deep, lasting impression on us, even if our time with them is brief. For us, that was our mother, Joan (Jo) Ellen Denton Meador. She was always so full of life and even when bad news came along, she stood up and was ready to face it head-on.

Our mother was diagnosed with breast cancer at the age of 33 and fought the battle for 13 years. We know there were times when she wanted to give up, but she always fought to be there with us.

Mom was the best cook we knew and made so many great meals that to this day there are certain things we just won't eat because we know it's "not like Mom's." She was a great woman and will always be the best mother we ever knew. We all love you, Mom, and await the day when we will see you again.

– From loving children Kelsey, Halee, and Andrew Meador

Beef Brisket

$\frac{1}{3}$ C. lemon juice
1 can beef broth
$\frac{1}{2}$ bottle liquid smoke
Small bottle soy sauce
$\frac{1}{4}$ t. garlic powder
$\frac{1}{4}$ t. pepper
3-5 lbs. beef brisket

- Mix all ingredients together and pour over brisket inside a baking bag.
- Seal bag, place in refrigerator and marinate the brisket for at least 24 hours.
- Place baking bag with brisket in a large roasting pan and cook for 5-6 hours at 275°.

– Recipe from the Kitchen of Joan Ellen Denton Meador

"Home is where your mother is!"

Janie Mika

I was only 23 years old and eight months pregnant with my first child when I lost my mother, Caryl Jane Mika, to breast cancer four years ago. She was only 48.

When she was first diagnosed and went through chemotherapy and radiation, her cancer was at stage three. Two

years later, it had metastasized to her liver and she died within two weeks. I was very overwhelmed – suddenly my world had turned upside down. I knew I had to go on for my baby and my family. After all, it was my mother who had shown me strength by example when her own mother had died only a month earlier. I remember my mom saying how strange it felt to no longer have a mother here on earth. I would sadly understand that feeling all too soon myself.

It hasn't been easy; I miss her every day. What hurts the most is that she never got to meet my daughter, her first grandchild. I don't think that Kailey resembles my mother physically, but her actions and mannerisms are the same. I guess that is how part of us sticks around even after we are gone.

I had a hard time picking the perfect recipe to best represent my mother. I will always remember her making her favorite "Chocolate and Cherries Cake" at Christmas every year. This Christmas, I think I will honor my mother and make her famous cake with my own daughter.

– From loving daughter,
Sarah Guardiola

Chocolate and Cherries Cake

1 package of chocolate cake mix
1 6-oz. package semi-sweet chocolate chips
1 14-oz. can sweetened condensed milk
1 21-oz. can cherry pie filling, drained and chilled
   (reserve ½ C. sauce)
½ t. almond extract

- Preheat oven to 350°.
- Prepare and bake cake as package directs for two 9" round cake pans. Remove cakes from pans and cool thoroughly.
- In saucepan over medium-low heat, add the chocolate chips to the sweetened condensed milk. Combine and cook, stirring, until chips melt and mixture thickens (about 10 minutes).
- In a medium bowl, combine the cherries, reserved cherry sauce and almond extract.

Place one cake on a serving platter and top with half the chocolate mixture and then the cherries. Place the second cake on top of the first and cover with remaining chocolate mixture. Enjoy!

– Recipe from the Kitchen of Janie Mika

Judith Milbourn

This cake is my absolute favorite! I can't remember when my mom started making it, but she made it once for my birthday and it has been "my birthday cake" ever since. My mom used to make it for me every year, and now my husband and children have taken over the tradition. This recipe holds such fond memories of Mom and the time she spent making it for my birthdays. It's not a hard cake to make, just a little time-consuming, but is well worth it!

Everything my mom made, she made with love and care. She thoroughly enjoyed cooking, and it showed. I miss her very much!

– From loving daughter,
Katrina Westbrook

German Chocolate Torte Cake

German Chocolate cake mix
²/₃ C. sugar
1 t. vanilla
8 oz. cream cheese
¼ t. cinnamon
8 oz. sour cream
¹/₃ C. chopped maraschino cherries (plus extra)
¾ C. grated chocolate bar (plus extra)
1½ C. whipped cream

- Prepare cake mix per the package instructions. Pour evenly into two 9" round cake pans. When done, cut each cake in half horizontally so that you have 4 cakes.
- Beat together the sugar, vanilla, cream cheese, cinnamon and sour cream until smooth. Add the cherries and grated chocolate, then fold in the whipped cream.
- Spread icing between all layers and frost top and sides. Sprinkle with grated chocolate on top and add a few whole cherries for decoration. Keep this cake refrigerated.

– Recipe from the Kitchen of Judith Milbourn

*"God could not be everywhere
and therefore He made mothers."*

– Jewish Proverb

Kathern E. Mock

My mother passed away after suffering with breast cancer for 12 years. Our family missed her greatly, but would not have wished her back with all the misery she had endured.

Mother was famous at church for her delicious apple pies, with their flaky crusts and yummy cinnamon flavor, and I was proud to serve her pies at the Beta Sigma Phi meetings in my home. However, no one has ever been able to duplicate her special touch with these wonderful desserts.

Having gone through the Depression, we were among the fortunate folks who never went hungry due to our father's beautiful vegetable gardens (which he kept even before and after WWII "victory gardens") and our mother's canning talents. Mother often said that when we were the poorest, our meals were the best – including everything from green beans to tomatoes, carrots, apples, peaches, raspberries and blackberries.

One of Mother's special recipes was her pickled beets, which make a great side dish. This is the recipe I wish to share with you and is one I frequently keep on hand to fill out our own family meals.

– From loving daughter,
Dolores "Dee" Van Dorn

Grandma Mock's Beets

3 C. vinegar
3 C. water
3 C. sugar
1 stick cinnamon
1 T. ground allspice
1 gallon prepared beets

- In a large pot, combine the vinegar, water, sugar, cinnamon and allspice. Heat to boiling and pour over the beets. (It is not necessary to use an entire gallon of beets. I frequently use canned beets and use the beet juice in place of the water.)

In addition, it was an Easter tradition in our family to add hard-boiled eggs to the beet juice and let set overnight in the refrigerator. This was a Pennsylvania Dutch recipe handed down over the years from our ancestors.

– Recipe from the Kitchen of Kathern E. Mock

Everybody knows that a good mother gives her children a feeling of trust and stability. She is their earth. She is the one they can count on for the things that matter most of all. She is their food and their bed and the extra blanket when it grows cold in the night. She is their warmth and their health and their shelter. She is the one they want to be near when they cry. She is the only person in the whole world in a whole lifetime who can be these things to her children. There is no substitute for her. Somehow even her clothes feel different to her children's hands from anybody else's clothes. Only to touch her skirt or her sleeve makes a troubled child feel better.

– Katharine Butler Hathaway

In 1970, after suffering for over five years with her disease, my mother died of cancer that had spread to every organ of her body but her heart. I was 24 with a five-year-old child, divorced and alone when she died. How I have missed her over the years, but consider myself very blessed to have had those 24 years with her.

Mom had a green thumb and loved gardening (especially growing dahlias), cooking and baking. I will always remember this favorite recipe of hers, "Cherry Coconut Cake," which she baked for my father every year on his birthday and on Easter. He so looked forward to this cake! She made it from scratch, but I have added a few modern "shortcuts." When I eat this cake, I don't count calories – I think of Mom.

– From loving daughter,
Carol Underwood

Cherry Coconut Cake

1 white cake mix
¼ C. maraschino cherry juice
½ C. chopped maraschino cherries (plus extra for garnish)
½ C. chopped walnuts (plus extra for garnish)
Seven-Minute Frosting (recipe follows)
½ C. flaked coconut

- Prepare cake mix according to directions, except take out ¼ C. of water and substitute with maraschino cherry juice (this makes the cake a nice pink color).
- Stir the cherries and walnuts into the cake batter, and pour into two greased and floured 9" or 10" cake pans. Bake until toothpick comes out clean (following directions on the cake mix box).
- Ice cake with frosting and cover lightly with the coconut, sprinkling some chopped cherries and walnuts on top. This is a beautiful cake and has a great taste.

(Continued...)

Seven-Minute Frosting

1½ C. sugar
½ t. cream of tartar
½ t. salt
½ C. water
1½ T. corn syrup
2 egg whites
½ t. vanilla

- Place the sugar, cream of tartar, salt, water and corn syrup in a saucepan and cook over medium heat until well dissolved. Set aside.
- In a medium glass mixing bowl, beat the egg whites to stiff peaks with an electric mixer and slowly fold in the vanilla flavoring.
- Pour the hot mixture very slowly into the egg whites and continue beating for five minutes. Let cool slightly before frosting cake.

– Recipe from the Kitchen of Eleanor Weaver Montgomery

Carla Morasca

My mom started making "Bunny Bread" when I was little, always around Easter time. I remember smelling the bread baking in the oven when I was playing outside as a kid, and would go running into the house to get a piece.

She actually found this recipe in a newspaper, and thought making the bread shaped like a bunny would be a fun twist on the normal braided Easter loaf. My mother *loved* to cook and try new recipes, so this was a fun challenge for her. It turned out great and has been a favorite in our family ever since!

Eventually Mom got me involved in the baking, which is a fond memory of mine. I always got to put the eyes and teeth on the bunny – it's so cute and charming when it is finished (and tastes great!). I loved the bread so much that we started making it all year round, not just at Easter.

Every time I smell sweet dough baking, I think of my mom and the fun she, Dad and I would have around the kitchen making "Bunny Bread."

– From loving daughter,
Jenna Morasca

Bunny Bread

Sweet Bread

1 C. sugar
1 T. salt
3 packages active dry yeast
8 - 9 C. all-purpose flour
2 C. milk
1 C. butter
2 eggs
Touch of vanilla (*optional – added by my mom*)
Raisins
Almonds
1 egg

- In a large mixing bowl, combine the sugar, salt, yeast and 2 C. flour.
- In a 2-quart saucepan over low heat, slowly heat the milk and butter until very warm, about 125 - 130° (the butter does not need to melt).
- With a mixer on low speed, gradually beat the milk and butter mixture into the dry ingredients.
- Increase mixer speed to medium and beat for 2 more minutes, scraping bowl occasionally with rubber spatula.
- Beat in the eggs (and vanilla, if desired) and 2 C. flour. Continue beating for 2 minutes. With a spoon, stir in enough additional flour (about 4 ¼ C) to make a soft dough.
- Turn dough onto lightly floured surface. Knead until smooth and elastic, about 10 minutes. Shape into a ball.
- Turn over in a large, oiled bowl to grease the top. Cover and let rise in a warm place until double in size (about 1 hour).
- Punch down dough. On lightly floured surface, divide into pieces according to your desired bread shape. Cover and let rest for 15 minutes.

(Continued...)

99

Easter Bunny

- Use 21 rolled dough balls. If the dough is frozen, thaw until soft.
- Use nine rolls for the bunny's body. Knead together and form into an egg shape.
- Use six rolls for the head and form into a ball.
- Use one roll for each lower paw.
- Use ½ roll for upper paws; form into fan-shaped balls and cut three "fingers."
- Use one roll per ear. Roll into a 12" rope, fold in half and place near the head, tucking ends under head.
- Face: Use ¼ roll for each cheek. Use less than 1/8 roll for nose. Use raisins for eyes. Cut one whole blanched almond in half for teeth.
- Brush everything with whole beaten egg, including teeth. Let rise until double (about 1 hour). Bake at 350° for 25-30 minutes, or until lightly browned.

– Recipe from the Kitchen of Carla Morasca

Debbie Nickell

Debbie Nickell was a wonderful mom, the very best anyone could have. Not only was she a wonderful cook, she was a wonderful friend, wife and mother. Anyone who visited would be invited to sit down at the kitchen table and, before you knew it, there would be a feast in front of you! Friends, acquaintances and strangers alike would come over just to talk and, of course, to eat. She taught me how to be the woman I am, the cook I am, and the mother I am today.

– From loving daughter,
Lori James

"A mother is someone who dreams great dreams for you, but then lets you chase the dreams you have for yourself and loves you just the same."

– Anonymous

Spam Sandwiches

1 onion, chopped
1 can Spam
1 can cream of mushroom soup
1 lb. Velveeta cheese, grated
12-18 dinner rolls

- Mix together the onion, Spam, soup and cheese.
- Make a small hole in the bottom of each roll and scoop out the insides.
- Pack the Spam mixture into the hollowed-out rolls and seal each one back up with a small piece of bread.
- Wrap the sandwiches in foil and bake at 350° for about 45 minutes, or until heated through.

– Recipe from the Kitchen of Debbie Nickell

Joan O'Neill

Coming home to the garlicky smell of this delicious soup definitely improved my outlook and my dad's on the day at hand. My mom was a wonderful cook (of everything), and she could make this soup like nobody else. It's funny – when you lose someone you love, there are so many little things that you miss which remind you of them every day. Mom was a wonderful lady and an incredible mother.

– From loving daughter,
Jenn O'Neill

Spud Special

4½ T. butter
1½ minced garlic cloves
1½ C. chopped onions
¾ C. chopped celery
1½ t. minced parsley
2¼ t. salt
⅜ t. black pepper
6 C. diced potatoes
3 C. chicken stock
3 C. milk

- Melt the butter in a large stockpot. Add the garlic and stir for 30 seconds over medium-high heat.
- Add the onions, celery and parsley, and sauté until vegetables soften. Add the salt and pepper and stir to blend.
- Add the potatoes and chicken stock and simmer over medium heat until the potatoes are well cooked. Stir in the milk.
- Heat thoroughly and enjoy!

– Recipe from the Kitchen of Joan O'Neill

*"A mother holds her children's hands
for awhile, but their hearts forever."*

Sue Johnston
Patterson

My mom died a long time ago, when I was a little girl. I have memories of Mom bowling, sewing (dresses for my sisters and me, and outfits for our Barbie dolls), and baking – she was a great cook.

The picture I've chosen is of Mom posing in the new kitchen that was added on to our house – she was so happy with that kitchen. Unfortunately, she didn't get to spend much time in it before she died at age 34 from breast cancer, leaving seven young children behind.

"Peanut Butter Bars" is probably the most beloved and popular of Mom's recipes. At least it is the one that shows up most frequently at family gatherings. Even my brother bakes them – at one of our family celebrations, four siblings all ended up bringing "Peanut Butter Bars"! Interestingly, each batch tasted just a little different – one had more topping; one was a little crunchier; one had a thicker layer of chocolate chips; and one had no chocolate chip layer at all – and each was equally good. I guess there's just no way to mess up "Peanut Butter Bars"!

– From loving daughter,
Hilah (Suzy) Perkin

Peanut Butter Bars

½ C. butter (or margarine)
½ C. granulated sugar
½ C. brown sugar
1 egg
⅓ C. peanut butter
½ t. baking soda
½ t. salt
½ t. vanilla
1 C. all-purpose flour
1 C. oats
6 oz. semi-sweet chocolate chips (more if desired)
½ C. powdered sugar
½ C. peanut butter
4-8 T. milk

- Preheat oven to 350°.
- Cream the butter in a mixing bowl. Add the sugars and blend well.
- Blend in the egg, 1/3 C. peanut butter, baking soda, salt, and vanilla. Gradually blend in the flour and oats.
- Spread in a greased 9"x 13" baking pan and bake for 20 - 25 minutes.
- Remove from oven and sprinkle with the chocolate chips while still warm. Let stand 5 minutes, then gently smooth out the melted chips.
- In a separate mixing bowl, blend together the powdered sugar and ½ C. peanut butter. Add milk until just the right consistency to drizzle over the bars.
- Drizzle powdered sugar mixture over the cooled peanut butter bars and enjoy!

– Recipe from the Kitchen of Sue Johnston Patterson

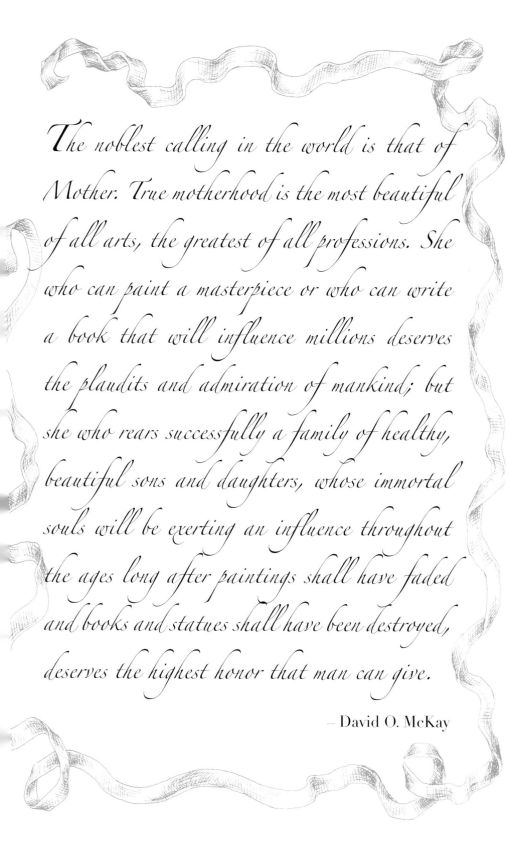

The noblest calling in the world is that of Mother. True motherhood is the most beautiful of all arts, the greatest of all professions. She who can paint a masterpiece or who can write a book that will influence millions deserves the plaudits and admiration of mankind; but she who rears successfully a family of healthy, beautiful sons and daughters, whose immortal souls will be exerting an influence throughout the ages long after paintings shall have faded and books and statues shall have been destroyed, deserves the highest honor that man can give.

– David O. McKay

Elizabeth Walter
Porter

When Mom could no longer bake, she asked me to make these cookies. When she saw them after they were baked, her comment was, "They look different than my cookies." After much discussion, we decided it was because she always mixed them by hand. Therefore, do not use an electric mixer for this recipe.

This recipe is a shortcut for a Dutch cookie recipe my grandma used to make. The original recipe called for ½ gallon of molasses, 2 cups of lard, 12 cups of flour, etc – such large quantities it had to be made in a dishpan!

Mom's greatest pleasure was making quilts, crafts and crocheted items to give as gifts. Her goal was to live to be 80 years old. Breast cancer took her life on January 29, 2002 – she would have been 80 on March 1 of that year.

– From loving daughter,
Linda Cash

Spicy Raisin Cookies

1 C. raisins
1 C. granulated sugar
1 C. brown sugar
¼ C. butter, or lard
2 eggs
2 T. molasses, light or dark (can substitute milk for
   the molasses)
2½ C. flour
1 t. baking soda
1 t. ground cinnamon
1 t. ground nutmeg
½ t. ground cloves

- Preheat oven to 350°.
- Heat raisins in a little water on stove until plump; drain and set aside.
- In a large mixing bowl, cream together the sugars and butter. Add the eggs and molasses and blend well.
- In a medium bowl, combine the flour, baking soda and spices and add to the creamed mixture. Stir by hand to blend.
- Shape into balls and bake on ungreased cookie sheets for 10 minutes.

– Recipe from the Kitchen of Elizabeth Walter Porter

Billie Jean
Riggs

My mother, Billie Jean Riggs, always made this cranberry salad at Thanksgiving and/or Christmas. I grew up eating this version and always loved it. Of course, I love anything and everything "cranberry," probably due to this very recipe!

– From loving daughter,
Marsha Ward

Cranberry Salad

2 C. cranberries (one pkg. fresh), coarsely chopped
1 C. sugar
1 C. seedless red grapes, cut in half
1 C. English walnuts or pecans, coarsely chopped
   (measure before chopping)
1 small tub of whipped topping

- Cover coarsely chopped cranberries with sugar and let sit overnight in a covered container.
- Mix with grapes, nuts and whipped topping. Chill and serve.

– Recipe from the Kitchen of Billie Jean Riggs

"Mother is the name for God in the lips and hearts of little children."

– William Makepeace Thackeray

Libby Ross

One of the fondest memories I have of my mother is her mouth-watering Southern cooking. Not only was she an amazing cook, but every ingredient and stir of the spoon was filled with warmth, caring and love for all those who passed through our kitchen. This recipe has special meaning to me, as I was a freshman in college, home for the weekend, when my mother taught me how to make this casserole. As she cut and shredded, we talked about boys, classes and my future. She always did know best, as you will discover in this tasty dish.

– From loving daughter,
Lori Ross

Southern Broccoli Casserole

1 C. cooked white rice
2½ C. steamed broccoli, cut into pieces
2 C. mild cheddar cheese, cubed
1 10¾-oz. can cream of mushroom soup
½ C. water
Salt
Pepper
½ C. mild cheddar cheese, shredded

- Preheat oven to 350°.
- Lightly coat an 8" x 8" x 2" glass baking dish with nonstick cooking spray.
- In a medium bowl, mix together the hot cooked rice, steamed broccoli and cubed cheddar cheese until most of the cheese is melted. Add the cream of mushroom soup, water, and salt & pepper to taste. Stir to combine.
- Spread broccoli mixture evenly into the baking dish. Sprinkle the top of the casserole with the shredded cheddar cheese.
- Bake for 25-30 minutes, until casserole is hot and cheese is bubbling. Serves 4.

– Recipe from the Kitchen of Libby Ross

Sally Sirico

My mother was only 56 years old when I lost her to breast cancer. She never had the opportunity to know me as an adult or to share in the joys of her grandchildren. My brother and I both agree that our Dad was the better cook in the family; Mom always took the shortcut and fixed dinners that were quick and easy, but still good. Here are two of my favorites from my mother, which I still serve today.

– From loving daughter,
Sally Goss

Golden Parmesan Sole

4 sole filets, fresh or frozen
½ C. butter or margarine, softened
1 C. Parmesan cheese

- Preheat oven to 400°.
- If using frozen filets, defrost first.
- Spread half the butter thickly over the bottom of a shallow baking dish. Sprinkle with half the cheese.
- Clean fish and dry well with paper towels. Arrange in a single layer over the butter and cheese. Dot with the remaining butter and sprinkle with the remaining cheese.
- Bake about 15 minutes, basting several times with pan juices, until flesh barely separates when tested with a knife.
- Pour drippings over fish before serving. Makes 4 servings.

This is a quick and easy dish for company. During baking, the cheese and butter brown slightly to a fine, thin crispness.

(Continued...)

Garlicky Tomatoes

2 medium tomatoes, halved
1 garlic clove, chopped
1 t. dried oregano
Salt and pepper, to taste
2 t. olive oil

- Place oven rack in top position and heat broiler.
- Place tomatoes cut side up on baking sheet. (Hint: If tomatoes wobble, cut thin slice off the bottoms so they'll sit flat on the baking sheet.)
- Divide the chopped garlic into 4 portions and place 1 portion on top of each tomato half. Sprinkle each half with oregano, salt, pepper and ½ t. olive oil.
- Broil tomatoes for about 5 minutes, or until the olive oil bubbles and tomatoes begin to soften. Serve immediately or refrigerate and serve cold. Makes 2 servings.

– Recipes from the Kitchen of Sally Sirico

Inez Smith

While I don't remember exactly when my mother started making this recipe, I can recall her making it with greater frequency once she realized that I liked it. I was a pretty picky eater as a child, so if there was something that I enjoyed, she did what she could to make it as often as possible. I remember disliking *kugel* when I was younger. In high school, however, I went to a restaurant with my mom and one of her friends and the restaurant served a *kugel* that smelled great. Soon after, my mom made this "Apricot Noodle Kugel," and I loved it.

I always phoned my mom for advice whenever I was sick, needed a recipe, or wanted to get stains out of clothing. Throughout my adult life, anytime I needed a dish for a potluck supper or party, I would call Mom for this recipe. It has always been a crowd pleaser, which pleased her.

Though she had taken care of people her whole life, Mom was forced to accept help from others at the end. The last night that I saw her, 10 days before she died, my mom told my dad, my brother, and me that she was frustrated – she had dreamed that she was able to cook and walk around the house and all she wanted was to wake up in the morning and make my dad breakfast. My mom died at  home on May 13, 2005, after fighting cancer for 2½ years. However, she got to see all of her children get married, witnessed seven grandchildren come into this world, and, as my dad says, accomplished all of her life goals. She touched many lives and continues to impact the choices that I make daily.

– From loving daughter,
Debra Hornbecker

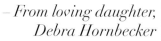

Apricot Noodle Kugel

A "kugel" is a crusty baked pudding made of potatoes or noodles.

8 oz. egg noodles
3 oz. cream cheese, softened
3 eggs, beaten
¼ C. butter, melted
1 t. vanilla
2 T. apricot jam
½ C. sugar
1 C. apricot juice
1 C. milk

Topping

1½ C. cornflakes, crushed
½ C. butter, melted
¼ C. sugar
1 t. cinnamon

- Grease a 9" x 9" baking dish and preheat oven to 350°.
- Bring a large saucepan full of water to boil and add the egg noodles; boil for 8 to 10 minutes. Drain noodles and set aside.
- Mix remaining *kugel* ingredients together in a large bowl. (It is okay if they are not perfectly blended.)
- Add the drained noodles and mix together using your hands until well blended. Pour into baking dish.
- Blend the topping ingredients together. Spread over topping over the noodles and bake for approximately 45 minutes, or until mixture is bubbling. Cool for 30 minutes before serving. Enjoy!

– Recipe from the Kitchen of Inez Smith

A mother is the truest friend we have. When trials heavy and sudden fall upon us, when adversity takes the place of prosperity, when friends who rejoice with us in our sunshine desert us, when troubles thicken around us, still will she cling to us and endeavor by her kind precepts and counsels to dissipate the clouds of darkness, and cause peace to return to our hearts.

– Washington Irving

Clara Squires

In November 1949, Clara Squires received a letter telling her that a three-month-old baby girl needed a home. Even though their three children were 11, 13 and 15 years old and life was not easy on a small north Missouri farm, Clara and her husband, Gordon, agreed to welcome this baby into their home to love as their own. I was that baby girl.

Mom's heart was full of love for her children and her kitchen was always filled with the aromas of home cooking. My favorite was her macaroon cookies. In 1965, Mom was diagnosed with lymphoma, and shortly thereafter with breast cancer. She lost her battle to cancer in May 1970, thirteen days before my first child was born.

The love she gave me has always set a pattern for the love I have for my sons. When my youngest son was born, a dear friend baked "Mom's Macaroons" and brought them to me in the hospital. When I opened the box and smelled those cookies, I knew Mom was smiling down on our new baby.

– From loving daughter,
B.J. Jones

Mom's Macaroons

1 C. granulated sugar
1 C. brown sugar
1 C. shortening
2 eggs
1 t. vanilla
2 C. flour
1 t. baking powder
1 t. baking soda
2 C. corn flakes
2 C. flaked coconut

- Preheat oven to 350°.
- In a large mixing bowl, cream together the sugars, shortening, eggs and vanilla.
- In a separate bowl, sift together the flour, baking powder and baking soda. Stir the dry ingredients into the creamed mixture.
- When well blended, add the corn flakes and coconut. Mix well and drop by teaspoonfuls on a lightly greased baking sheet.
- Bake for 10 minutes; remove to wire racks to cool.

– Recipe from the Kitchen of Clara Squires

Barbara Stabler

My mom, Barbara Stabler, was 48 when she was taken by breast cancer. Her own mother later succumbed to this dreaded disease at the age of 88. My mom was the oldest of three girls and both of her sisters have been diagnosed and undergone treatments for breast cancer over the past few years. I was 29 when my mom died. My kids never got to meet her, but they know all of the great stories of her life.

I chose this recipe for my grandmother's "Blueberry-Banana Muffins" for two reasons. First, my grandmother and I were very close up until the day she died. She was very much like

a mother to my family and me. Grandmother baked nonstop for everybody and everything, and always made sure that every sick friend and church bake sale had more food than they knew what to do with.

The second reason is that my mother loved the color blue. She even had a "Blue Room" in her home; everything in it was blue except for a white ceramic statue of a seagull I had made for her years ago. Though my mom and I had been estranged for some time during my teenage years, we made peace when I got a little older and I loved to go visit, sit and talk with her. One of my most treasured memories is of being in that room on my wedding day. The phones were ringing, people were at both doors, the dogs were barking, family and friends were scurrying about, and I stood alone in that "Blue Room" and just felt such great peace. I often close my eyes and go back there, especially when I'm baking "Blueberry-Banana Muffins."

— *From loving daughter,*
Kim Wedgerfield

Blueberry-Banana Muffins

¾ C. mashed bananas
½ C. white sugar
½ C. vegetable oil
2 eggs
1 t. vanilla
1¼ C. flour
1 t. baking powder
1 t. baking soda
½ C. oatmeal
¼ C. plain yogurt, or sour cream
½ C. blueberries, or more – up to one cup

- Preheat oven to 375°.
- Grease muffin tins or line with baking cups.
- In a medium mixing bowl, beat together the bananas, sugar, oil, eggs and vanilla.
- In a large mixing bowl, combine the flour, baking powder , baking soda and oatmeal. Add the banana mixture and stir to blend.
- Fold in the yogurt and blueberries. Pour batter into muffin tins and bake for 20 minutes.

– Recipe from the Kitchens of Louise Martin (grandmother)
and Barbara Stabler

Audrey Evelyn Steeden

I lost my mother to breast cancer in 1975 at the age of 50. My parents had been foster parents for 28 years and had cared for 423 babies and 63 teenagers over the years. I also have three adopted brothers.

When Mom passed away, my parents still had three small foster children in their home. I lived in Winnipeg, Manitoba, at the time and my parents were in Portage la Prairie. My sorority chapter made a lovely donation to a bursary that was started through the Children's Aid Society. The support from my sisters helped ease the pain and I will forever be grateful.

"Reindeer Candy" is a recipe that was passed down for generations in our family, and it was always made together as a family. Dad had to help in the stirring and Mom entertained us with Christmas stories to help the time pass more quickly. Dad would also manage to sneak us a taste while Mom was out of the room. Enjoy!

*– From loving daughter,
Beverly Robertson*

Reindeer Candy

1 can sweetened condensed milk
1 C. corn syrup
1 C. butter (*not* margarine)
1¼ C. brown sugar

- Place all ingredients in a saucepan and boil for approximately ½ hour, stirring constantly. (Do not beat!)
- Pour onto a large buttered cookie sheet when mixture reaches the hard-ball stage.
- Cool before breaking into pieces to serve.

This candy burns very easily so be sure to keep well stirred.

– Recipe from the Kitchen of Audrey Evelyn Steeden

"Youth fades, love droops, the leaves of friendship fall; a mother's secret hope outlives them all."

– Oliver Wendell Holmes

Betty Thomson

My mother was the most wonderful cook, and the kitchen was our favorite room in the house. In winter it was the warmest room, filled with the aroma of homemade cinnamon rolls or Christmas fudge. In summer there were fresh tomatoes from the garden ripening on the counters, just waiting to be sliced. So many memories of the meals I shared with my mother live on through my senses and come back to me every time I make one of her special dishes.

– From loving daughter,
Barbara Thomson

Pecan Hot Dip

8 oz. cream cheese
2 T. milk
½ C. sour cream
¼ C. chopped onion
½ T. garlic salt
2½-oz. jar dried beef
½ C. chopped pecans (may be heated first with 2 t. butter and ½ t. salt)

- Mix together the first 5 ingredients, then fold in the beef.
- Place in an 8" pie plate and sprinkle with the pecans.
- Bake at 350 degrees for 20 minutes, or until mixture is bubbling.

– Recipe from the Kitchen of Betty Thomson

Minnie Margaret Trevisan

My mother, Minnie Margaret Trevisan, died of breast cancer at the age of 41. I had just turned twelve years old. She was the mother of seven children, ages three to fifteen – four boys and three girls. I was third in line, but the oldest girl. I always felt like a little mother to my four younger siblings. I don't have many memories of my mom…sad, but true.

My father, Albert J. Trevisan, had died suddenly of a heart attack two months before my mom's death, and my siblings and I were subsequently raised by two sets of aunts and uncles at different times. Remarkably, we all got to stay together.

When I turned nineteen, I became the caregiver to my two younger brothers and two younger sisters. We had a house built and I was in charge of their care for the next three-and-a-half years. I did all of the cooking, shopping and bill paying. Every other month, when I got the bill from "The Edison Company," a recipe would be included with it. I eagerly tried each new recipe on my siblings.

"Chicken Tortilla Casserole" became our family favorite – everyone loves it! To this day I still make it for our family get-togethers. With my own children it has come to be a family tradition to have "Chicken Tortilla Casserole" on Christmas Eve every year. So, in honor of my mom, I share this wonderful recipe with you to enjoy. I hope it will become a family favorite of yours, too!

– From loving daughter,
Casey Enda

Chicken Tortilla Casserole

4 whole chicken breasts
Salt and pepper
½ C. water
1 C. chicken broth (see method below)
1 10½-oz. can cream of mushroom soup
2 7-oz. cans green chile salsa
1 C. milk
1 package corn tortillas, cut into 1" square pieces
1 can sliced black olives
1 lb. shredded cheddar cheese
1 T. chopped onion

- Place the chicken in large pot with a tight fitting lid. Season with salt and pepper to taste.
- Add water, cover tightly, and bring to a boil. Lower heat and simmer until tender, about 1 hour.
- Remove from heat and let chicken cool; reserve cooking broth (adding enough water, if needed, to make 1 C.). Cut chicken into bite-size pieces and set aside.
- Mix together 1 C. reserved broth, soup, salsa and milk. Set aside.
- Arrange half the tortillas in a buttered 13" x 9" x 2" casserole dish. Top with half the chicken and half the olives. Repeat.
- Pour soup mixture over the chicken and top with the cheese and onion. Refrigerate for several hours or overnight.
- Bake in a 350° oven, uncovered, for 1 hour, or until heated through. Makes 8 to 10 servings. Enjoy!

– Recipe from the Kitchen of Minnie Margaret Trevisan

A mother seems to specialize in doing thoughtful deeds;

Before you ask she understands your problems and your needs.

Quietly she does her best to help, inspire and cheer,

And everything looks brighter right away because she's near.

She always has a lot to do but still finds time to spare,

To listen and to give advice because she really cares.

She helps because she wants to; she finds joy in being kind,

And making others happy is the first thing on her mind.

She makes this world a better place by practicing the art

Of reaching out to others and by giving from the heart.

— Anonymous

Mary Elizabeth Vieira

My mother was born in 1909. As she grew up, she learned to cook the Azorean way. Cooking for 13 brothers and sisters was a good way to learn – they were always ready to be fed! Beans were and still are a staple of Portuguese cooking. We always ate our beans with a mild pork sausage called *linguica*.

This recipe was a favorite meal for my brother, David, and me. We always had a discussion about how much ketchup we judged to be just the right amount. Mom also made wonderful pies that my daughters still talk about to this day. Christmas time always meant pies, not cakes.

I am sharing my mother's bean recipe in celebration of her Portuguese heritage and her life.

– From loving daughter,
Arlene Mathias

Portuguese Beans

2½ C. dry pinto beans
Water

Sauce

6 slices bacon, chopped
½ chopped onion
2 cloves garlic, chopped
1 C. ketchup, or to taste
1 t. cinnamon
1 bay leaf
1 t. salt
⅛ t. cumin powder

- Rinse the beans and soak overnight, or bring to a boil for 1 minute and let sit 1 hour.
- Boil gently until cooked, perhaps 2 hours.
- Make sauce by first frying the bacon. Add the remaining ingredients and simmer gently (add a little water if sauce is too thick).
- Add sauce to cooked beans and enjoy!

(Variation: Use chopped *linguica* instead of bacon; you may also add ¼ C. chopped bell pepper.)

– Recipe from the Kitchen of Mary Elizabeth Vieira

Frances Riley
West

It was always at Christmas time – I would come home from school and there, beside the doorstep in the snow, would be a box full of butter, sugar and whole raw almonds. A note usually accompanied the box requesting my mom to please make the sender a batch of her famous "Almond Rocha." My mom worked for Mountain Bell Telephone Company as a switchboard operator in our hometown of Forsythe, Montana (pop. 3,000), and everybody knew her, and her "Almond Rocha."

When she got home from work, out came the big, deep-dish cast iron skillet. I would start splitting the almonds by hand as the smell of melted butter permeated the air. Mom would stir the ingredients constantly until the mixture turned a toffee brown, then she would pour it onto a cookie sheet. Sometimes she would get tired of stirring and would let me step in, but only if I wore an oven mitt (in case of splatter, as the candy was cooked on high heat).

My mother was diagnosed with breast cancer when I was in the seventh grade, and she passed away between my freshman and sophomore years of high school on July 6, 1967 – I was only13 years old.

My brother and I happened to walk into a relative's house a while back and the smell of melted butter was in the air. We both looked at each other and, at the same time, said, "ALMOND ROCHA!"

– From loving daughter,
Lynette Riley Kyle

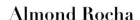

Almond Rocha

2 C. sugar
1 lb. butter, room temperature
1 C. split raw almonds
Several plain chocolate candy bars (optional)

- Put sugar, butter and almonds into a heavy-bottomed skillet. Break the butter into pieces so it will melt at the same rate as the sugar.
- Turn heat to high and stir continuously with a wooden spoon. The candy separates at first, but will form a creamy mass as you keep stirring.
- Watch carefully – when it starts to turn the color of a brown paper bag, remove the mixture from the heat and pour it onto an ungreased cookie sheet.
- Let cool and then break into pieces.

(Variation: You may place chocolate candy bars on the Almond Rocha while it is still warm. Let them melt and then spread the chocolate across the top with a spatula.)

– Recipe from the Kitchen of Frances Riley West

Kathleen Zinkgraf

My mom used to make this dish in the winter. I know it sounds awfully high in salt and fat, but it is yummy! This recipe is from back in the days when moms were using canned and prepared products to make speedy meals. My mom was all for that!

My mom learned to cook on her own as a teenager when her own mother passed away from ovarian cancer. Therefore, our meals were normally simple fare. This recipe was a fun one for our family dinners, which we ate together every day at 6:00 p.m. sharp.

– From loving daughter,
Candyce Kamphaus

Potato Chip Tuna Casserole

1-lb. bag of potato chips (*not* ruffled), $^2/_3$ crushed and
  $^1/_3$ uncrushed
2 cans of tuna, drained
2 cans cream of mushroom soup

- Preheat oven to 350°.
- Layer half the crushed chips in a greased casserole dish, followed by 1 can of tuna and 1 can of soup.
- Repeat with another layer of the crushed chips, 1 can of tuna and 1 can of soup.
- Bake for 20 minutes.
- Remove from oven and place the uncrushed potato chips on top of the casserole and return to oven until slightly brown.

– Recipe from the Kitchen of Kathleen Zinkgraf

*"Sometimes the poorest woman leaves
her children the richest inheritance."*

– Ruth E. Renkel

Arroline Zumbrunn

My mother, Arroline Zumbrunn, was an English teacher at Bonner Springs (Kansas) High School for 33 years before she retired in 1985. She and my father moved to Bonner Springs in the early 1950s and lived there the rest of their lives.

She was diagnosed in 1981 with breast cancer and had a mastectomy and many lymph nodes removed, followed by radiation and chemotherapy. Over the next five years, my mother had two more rounds of chemotherapy. Until the very end, she never gave up the fight and handled this disease with dignity and grace. She died in April 1986.

Although it has been 20 years since Mom's death, it sometimes seems like only yesterday that I was hanging out in her kitchen, visiting with her and doing all the dishes while she prepared one thing or another for a family gathering.

The recipe I have chosen is for cookies called "Peanut Blossoms." I remember my mother getting this recipe in the early 1960s from a friend and writing it by hand on a sheet of typing paper. That paper is now very old, yellowed, creased, and tattered. I keep it in a plastic sheet protector so it will not deteriorate further.

I recall it usually requiring twice as many candies as the recipe needed to ensure there were enough to top the cookies – my brother, sister, and I would always raid the candy sack while Mom was baking her "Peanut Blossoms"!

– From loving daughter,
Margene Swart

Peanut Blossoms

1¾ C. all purpose flour
1 t. baking soda
½ t. salt
½ C. shortening
½ C. peanut butter
½ C. sugar
½ C. firmly packed brown sugar
1 egg, unbeaten
2 T. milk
1 t. vanilla
Granulated sugar
1 bag chocolate candy kisses

- Preheat oven to 375°.
- In a medium bowl, sift together the flour, baking soda and salt.
- In a large mixing bowl, cream together the shortening and peanut butter. Gradually add the granulated and brown sugars, creaming well.
- Add the egg, milk and vanilla, and beat well.
- Gradually add the dry ingredients to the wet ingredients, mixing thoroughly.
- Shape by rounded teaspoonfuls into balls. Roll in sugar and place on ungreased cookie sheets.
- Bake for 8 minutes.
- Remove from oven and place a solid milk chocolate candy kiss on top of each cookie, pressing down so that cookie cracks around edges.
- Return to oven and bake 2-5 minutes longer. Remove cookies to wire racks to cool.

– Recipe from the Kitchen of Arroline Zumbrunn

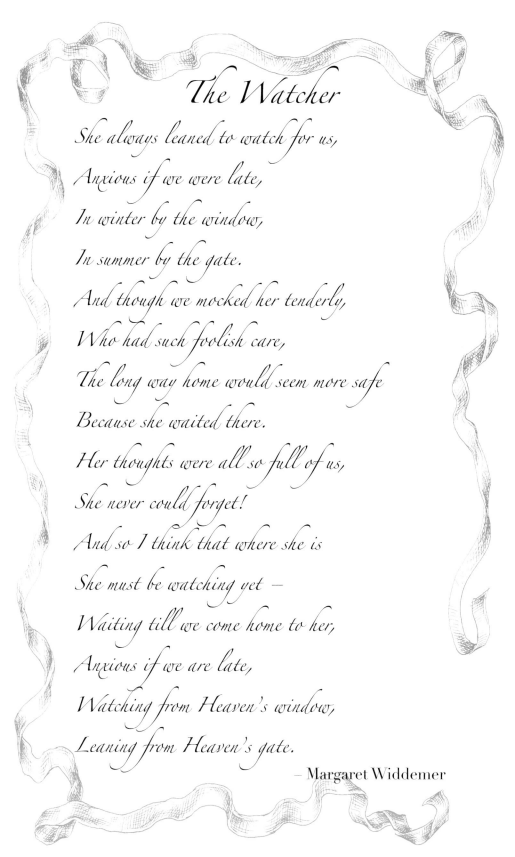

The Watcher

She always leaned to watch for us,

Anxious if we were late,

In winter by the window,

In summer by the gate.

And though we mocked her tenderly,

Who had such foolish care,

The long way home would seem more safe

Because she waited there.

Her thoughts were all so full of us,

She never could forget!

And so I think that where she is

She must be watching yet —

Waiting till we come home to her,

Anxious if we are late,

Watching from Heaven's window,

Leaning from Heaven's gate.

— Margaret Widdemer

LISA BURTON lives on a rural Kansas farm with her husband and a blended family of five children, three dogs, five cats, and two rabbits. In addition to promoting breast cancer awareness, her passions include antiquing, reading, "repurposing" found items, and sewing.

Lisa runs a Web-based business, **pinkribbonconnection.com**, specializing in handmade breast cancer awareness products.

For future editions of *Around My Mother's Table*, she is soliciting additional stories/recipes from children of mothers lost to breast cancer. Please contact her website for information on this and other projects.

Thank you for supporting breast cancer research through the purchase of this book.

Acknowledgments

I would like to express a deeply heartfelt thanks to my dad, Bob Durbin. Without his generous support and love, this project would not have been possible. Thank you, Dad – I love you!

Material quoted on page viii from *Motherless Daughters: The Legacy of Loss*, © 1994 by Hope Edelman, Addison-Wesley Publishing Company, Reading, Mass. Reprinted with permission.

Poem on page 175, "The Watcher," by Margaret Widdemer from *Cross Currents*, © 1921 by Harcourt, Brace and Company, Inc.